RAMAKRISHNA
ON NON-DOERSHIP

Gautam Sachdeva

YogiImpressions®

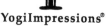

YogiImpressions®
RAMAKRISHNA ON NON-DOERSHIP
First published in India in 2017 by
Yogi Impressions Books Pvt. Ltd.
1711, Centre 1, World Trade Centre,
Cuffe Parade, Mumbai 400 005, India.
Website: www.yogiimpressions.com

First Edition, January 2017

Copyright © 2017 by Gautam Sachdeva

Quotes from *The Gospel of Sri Ramakrishna*
First published in the United States: 1942
by Swami Nikhilananda
Ramakrishna-Vivekananda Centre, New York

ISBN 978-93-82742-57-9

*Dedicated to all the spiritual masters
who have impacted my life*

Sant Dnyaneshwar[1]
(1275–1296)

Work or karma
Come to happen
The fool avers
'I' made it happen

Such insolent fools
Must never be shown
Karma's rules
And its tools

The wise watch karma
Notch upon notch
They witness karma's
Ticking watch

They are like the sun
Not touched by the earth
Like a witness to their bodies
They watch it run

Nature in its course
And man with his traits
Work comes to happen
By way of these traits

But those who think
It's they who work and act
Have twisted the facts
And are riddled with their acts

— *Dnyaneshwari* [2]

INTRODUCTION

The self, deluded by egoism, thinketh: 'I am the doer.'[3]
— *The Bhagavad Gita*

"Nobody truly 'does' anything. We are all instruments through whom the Divine Will functions. This is according to me the true meaning of 'universal brotherhood'; we are a brotherhood of instruments through whom God's Will functions."

This is what my spiritual guide and contemporary Advaita sage Ramesh Balsekar (1917-2009), spoke about at the daily talks that were held at his home in South Mumbai. He would explain in a step-by-step manner how he not only reached this conclusion based on his personal experience in daily living, but also how the same message was echoed in the Indian scriptures, as well as the teachings of the Buddha, Jesus, and 20th century masters like Sri Ramana Maharshi.

The deeds are, but no doer of the deeds is there...[4]
– Gautama Buddha

Actions form no bondage. Bondage is only the false notion,
'I am the doer.' Leave off such thoughts and let the body and
senses play their role, unimpeded by your interference.[5]
– Sri Ramana Maharshi

Mysterious is the path of action. Though I do nothing,
they hold Me responsible for the actions which take place
on account of prarabdha (destiny). I am only their witness.
The Lord is the sole doer and inspirer.[6]
– Shirdi Sai Baba

Ramesh would explain this ancient truth in simple terms
with reference to one's daily living. At the outset, he would
ask us to investigate the matter and state that upon doing so,
we would inevitably reach the conclusion that our actions
(what we 'did' or decided to 'do'), depend on our thoughts,
and nobody could know what the next thought was going to
be. If such was the case, then how could we call it 'our' action?

He would also explain how our actions were based on
something we saw, heard, tasted, touched, or smelt. And
none of these were in our control. For example, we saw
something because we were present at a certain place at a
certain time, and therefore happened to see it. This in turn
led to our action. If we were not there at a certain time and
place, our action could or would not have happened. More
importantly, something had to happen while we were there,
else our action would not have happened.

When Ramana Maharshi said words to the effect that there was truly no free will, someone put up his hand and said, "My putting up my hand is indeed my free will to do so." To this, Sri Ramana replied that if he had not said there was no free will, the individual concerned would not have put up his hand.

Our decisions, Ramesh would go on to say, are based on our genes and conditioning – neither of which were made by us or were in our control. We did not choose our genes, nor did we choose our environment – geographic, social, economic and so on – that formed the basis of our conditioning. We have been bombarded with conditioning from day one – at home, in the relevant society, in school and college, as well as conditioning in the church, mosque, or temple.

Therefore, is it really our 'doing' when there are so many factors involved that are beyond our control, which shape all our decisions – all that 'we' think we 'do'? Or, are we a part of the functioning of Totality, which causes to bring about exactly that what is supposed to be brought about in a given situation, at a particular moment in time?

Sathya Sai Baba had something pertinent to say on this subject, as can be seen from the extract below:

> "Now you might say, 'But I have free will. How can I just accept God's Will?' There are two ways of looking at that. One is, if you have been considering this whole problem for some time, you may understand that this world in which we live, is similar to a dream.

Swami (referring to Sathya Sai Baba) says so, the great sages of old say so. Do you remember what we said about your nighttime dream? You can ask yourself, suppose in the nighttime dream, you said that you have free will to do this or that? In the dream, free will has no meaning whatsoever, because when you awake, the dream disappears. Similarly, in this waking world, Swami says you *seem* to have free will, and you should act on that premise. You come to a decision, and then you engage in action – and you may feel that you are acting according to your will.

"After the action has taken place, you look back and say, 'Oh, I could have done it this way or that way instead and exercised my free will.' But the fact is that you acted in a certain way.

"What were the influences that caused you to act in that way? Were these influences your free will? No. Undoubtedly not. From the time you were born, you have been filled with influences and ideas from every direction…

"Now, when we decide on any course of action, we plan what we are going to do, but we cannot count on our plans being successful, can we? Very often it does not turn out the way we planned. So the factor that makes the result vary from our plans is the presence of the Lord in every action that we take. Swami says it is best to conclude that everything that happens is God's Will, and not struggle against it. Just accept it as God's Will and ask for God's Grace. He says that is the height, the summit of devotion."[7]

Coming back to Ramesh's talks, there were some seekers for whom what Ramesh said was an eye opener, while others took to it like a fish takes to water, and there were those who were rather aghast at the concept. After all, what would happen to one's free will and responsibility, if one did not 'do' anything? Of course, this was the natural defence of the ego as its most prized possession – its sense of doership – was under assault. The immediate response that would come up would be: 'Then what prevents me from picking up a machine gun and gunning down people?'

Ramesh would explain that that would not happen if it was not in one's nature to do so in the first place. And, more importantly, the concept of non-doership did not absolve individuals of their responsibility to society, which would certainly consider it as 'their' action and punish or reward them accordingly.

I found a certain peace in this teaching. If no one truly 'did' anything, then blame, condemnation, hate, malice, etc. went out of the window, as far as the actions of others were concerned. And so did pride, arrogance, guilt, and shame for one's own actions. An absence of all these meant – peace of mind. And this is precisely what enlightenment would give 'me' that I did not have before. Ramesh would make it clear that this was 'enlightened living'. He would say, "What would enlightenment give me that I didn't have before? It would certainly not enable me to walk on water, to be in two places at the same time, or find a parking spot whenever I needed it. All it would give me is peace of mind."

This is best summed up by Narendra (Swami Vivekananda) in *The Gospel of Sri Ramakrishna*:

"Realization depends on God's grace. Sri Krishna says in the *Gītā*: The Lord, O Arjuna, dwells in the hearts of all beings, causing them, by His māyā, to revolve as if mounted on a machine. Take refuge in Him with all thy heart, O Bhārata. By His grace wilt thou attain Supreme Peace and the Eternal Abode."[8]

Over the years that I spent with Ramesh, as a disciple as well as the publisher of some of his books, I got to understand his fondness for certain masters. Among them were contemporary Indian Advaita sages like Sri Ramana Maharshi and Ramesh's own guru Sri Nisargadatta Maharaj. He was also fond of the writings of the Irish mystic Terrence Gray, popularly known as 'Wei Wu Wei'. But what was more often than not missed by many was Ramesh's deep regard for Sri Ramakrishna Paramahamsa. In fact, Ramesh would utter the names '…Jesus, Buddha, Ramana Maharshi, Ramakrishna Paramahamsa' in the same breath.

Working with him while editing some of his books, I would unexpectedly find references to the sayings of Sri Ramakrishna. This was a departure as Ramakrishna was mostly considered a master of Bhakti Yoga, while Ramesh and his lineage and leanings were all centered on the Jnana Yoga path. Yet, the references to Ramakrishna and his sayings kept cropping up.

It was in January 2016 that I picked up *The Gospel of Sri Ramakrishna* to read. I had purchased this book at the Ramakrishna Ashram at Bellur Math, when I visited it some years back on an impromptu trip with my good friend Gabriel. As I went through the thick book, it dawned on me as to why Ramesh was so fond of the Paramahamsa's teachings. For there was so much that he said on non-doership, which echoed what Ramesh would say in his daily talks, or write about in his books. I kept underlining the references to non-doership as I read through the book.

It was after I finished reading it that I felt that, perhaps, the light this master has thrown on the subject could be collated into a small book, which would especially help today's seekers grasp the essence of his message on non-doership.

Of course, Ramesh's teaching was in a more modern idiom and he took the trouble to explain this lofty concept to seekers who were prone to questioning everything. Ramesh would welcome questions and dialogue on the subject as he knew the seekers visiting him had their cups already full with many concepts. Ramakrishna saying it, on the other hand, was readily accepted by his disciples as he was regarded as a 'divine incarnation'. At least this is what I observed upon reading *The Gospel of Sri Ramakrishna*, wherein there was very little questioning of the Avatar's words of wisdom.

Ramakrishna would repeatedly mention, "I am a machine and God is its operator." When I kept coming across this statement while I read the book, it reminded me of what Ramesh had mentioned in the Foreword of my first book *Pointers from Ramesh Balsekar*:

"To be told that he (Gautam) was more a machine than a man did not surprise him at all. And that reminds me of a story that I read a long time ago. A large multinational company had to engage a number of people at a fairly high level, and they wanted to be sure that there would not be the slightest prejudice in the selection and that the selection would be totally objective. So, they used a very expensive robot especially designed for the purpose.

"One particular candidate soon forgot that he was being interviewed by a robot and, while arguing a certain point, burst out saying, 'You are a fool!' The robot quietly replied, 'Maybe so, my friend, but it is you who is being interviewed for the job.' " [9]

The ultimate takeaway of the priceless gift of non-doership was that if nobody truly did anything then it could be clearly seen that, as Ramesh was famous for saying, "Consciousness is all there is... Consciousness is you, me, he and she."

Just as it is the same electricity that functions through all the gadgets in the kitchen, enabling each gadget to produce what it is designed to (and without which each gadget would be inoperative), in the same way we are all instruments through whom the same energy – Consciousness – functions. Each one of us is 'designed' (genes and conditioning) to think the way we think, feel the way we feel, and do the things we do. If that is so, then whom can one possibly hate? Consciousness? Can Consciousness hate Itself?

Inversely, whom can one possibly love if there is no 'other' to love? For, Consciousness by Its very nature is Love – not the dualistic love between two individuals, but the deeply intimate Love where there is no one as separate from the 'other' to love.

Readers of this book may find some of the extracts to be repetitive. These have been retained as, after all, Sri Ramakrishna kept repeating the same message to those who came to him. Ramesh would also repeat the same message in his daily talks. He would say, "The phenomenal conditioning of maya is so powerful that it needs the pounding to be done continuously by the guru in order to break it."

However, it is pertinent to note that although some quotes may appear repetitive, one can detect a subtle yet noticeable difference in their nuance. This can be observed in cases of certain other words or examples used by the master.

On a lighter note, I came across this dialogue by Ramakrishna towards the end of *The Gospel of Sri Ramakrishna*, which sheds light on his thoughts on repetition:

> "Hriday used to say to me: 'Uncle, please don't give out your stock of instructions all at once. Why should you repeat the same things over and over again?' I would reply: 'You fool, what's that to you? These are my words and if I like I shall repeat them a hundred thousand times. You keep quiet!'" [10]

If one accepts the concept of non-doership, the question

that arises is: 'I know that I am not the doer of my actions. But, how do I live my life knowing that I am not the doer?' As Ramesh would reply, "Act *as if* you're the doer, knowing that you are not."

Finally, when masters like Ramakrishna Paramahamsa consistently point to non-doership, it would help to listen to their words with an open mind, instead of the habituated mode of listening of the individual 'me', which is already equipped with an arsenal of questions, quick to refute, discard or disagree with what has just been heard or read. Rather, one should approach what is said with an openness that would allow the seeds of non-doership that have been planted to sprout in due course, enabling one to flow through life's brief journey with equanimity and peace of mind.

This is the spirit in which this book is offered to you.

Gautam Sachdeva
November 2016

Sri Ramakrishna Paramahansa
(1836–1886)

EXTRACTS

One day Girish felt depressed because he was unable to submit to any routine of spiritual discipline. In an exalted mood the Master said to him: "All right, give me your power of attorney. Henceforth I assume responsibility for you. You need not do anything." Girish heaved a sigh of relief. He felt happy to think that Sri Ramakrishna had assumed his spiritual responsibilities. But poor Girish could not then realize that he also, on his part, had to give up his freedom and make of himself a puppet in Sri Ramakrishna's hands. The Master began to discipline him according to this new attitude. One day Girish said about a trifling matter, "Yes, I shall do this." "No, no!" the Master corrected him. "You must not speak in that egotistic manner. You should say, 'God willing, I shall do it'." Girish understood. Thenceforth he tried to give up all idea of personal responsibility and surrender himself to the Divine Will. His mind began to dwell constantly on Sri Ramakrishna. This unconscious meditation in time chastened his turbulent spirit.

Master (*to Narendra*): "How do you feel about it? Worldly people say all kinds of things about the spiritually minded. But look here! When an elephant moves along the street, any number of curs and other small animals may bark and cry after it; but the elephant doesn't even look back at them. If people speak ill of you, what will you think of them?"

Narendra: "I shall think that dogs are barking at me."

Master (*smiling*): "Oh, no! You mustn't go that far, my child! (*Laughter.*) God dwells in all beings. But you may be intimate only with good people; you must keep away from the evil-minded. God is even in the tiger; but you cannot embrace the tiger on that account. (*Laughter.*) You may say, 'Why run away from a tiger, which is also a manifestation of God?' The answer to that is: 'Those who tell you to run away are also manifestations of God – and why shouldn't you listen to them?'

"Let me tell you a story. In a forest there lived a holy man who had many disciples. One day he taught them to see God in all beings and, knowing this, to bow low before them all. A disciple went to the forest to gather wood for the sacrificial fire. Suddenly he heard an outcry: 'Get out of the way!

A mad elephant is coming!' All but the disciple of the holy man took to their heels. He reasoned that the elephant was also God in another form. Then why should he run away from it? He stood still, bowed before the animal, and began to sing its praises. The māhut of the elephant was shouting: 'Run away! Run away!' But the disciple didn't move. The animal seized him with its trunk, cast him to one side, and went on its way. Hurt and bruised, the disciple lay unconscious on the ground. Hearing what had happened, his teacher and his brother disciples came to him and carried him to the hermitage. With the help of some medicine he soon regained consciousness. Someone asked him, 'You knew the elephant was coming – why didn't you leave the place?' 'But', he said, 'our teacher has told us that God Himself has taken all these forms, of animals as well as men. Therefore, thinking it was only the elephant God that was coming, I didn't run away.' At this the teacher said: 'Yes, my child, it is true that the elephant God was coming; but the māhut God forbade you to stay there. Since all are manifestations of God, why didn't you trust the māhut's words? You should have heeded the words of the māhut God.' (*Laughter.*)

"It is said in the scriptures that water is a form of God. But some water is fit to be used for worship, some water for washing the face, and some only for washing plates or dirty linen. This last sort cannot be used for drinking or for a holy purpose. In like manner, God undoubtedly dwells in the hearts of all – holy and unholy, righteous and unrighteous; but a man should not have dealings with the unholy, the wicked, the impure. He must not be intimate with them.

With some of them he may exchange words, but with others he shouldn't go even that far. He should keep aloof from such people."

A devotee: "Sir, if a wicked man is about to do harm, or actually does so, should we keep quiet then?"

Master: "A man living in society should make a show of tamas to protect himself from evil-minded people. But he should not harm anybody in anticipation of harm likely to be done him.

"Listen to a story. Some cowherd boys used to tend their cows in a meadow where a terrible poisonous snake lived. Everyone was on the alert for fear of it. One day a brahmachāri was going along the meadow. The boys ran to him and said: 'Revered sir, please don't go that way. A venomous snake lives over there.' 'What of it, my good children?' said the brahmachāri. 'I am not afraid of the snake. I know some mantras.' So saying, he continued on his way along the meadow. But the cowherd boys, being afraid, did not accompany him. In the mean time the snake moved swiftly toward him with upraised hood. As soon as it came near, he recited a mantra, and the snake lay at his feet like an earthworm. The brahmachāri said: 'Look here. Why do you go about doing harm? Come, I will give you a holy word. By repeating it you will learn to love God. Ultimately you will realize Him and so get rid of your violent nature.' Saying this, he taught the snake a holy word and initiated him into spiritual life. The snake bowed before the teacher and said, 'Revered sir, how shall I practise spiritual discipline?' 'Repeat that sacred word', said the teacher, 'and do no harm to anybody'. As he was about to depart, the brahmachāri said, 'I shall see you again.'

"Some days passed and the cowherd boys noticed that the snake would not bite. They threw stones at it. Still it showed no anger; it behaved as if it were an earthworm. One day one of the boys came close to it, caught it by the tail, and, whirling it round and round, dashed it again and again on the ground and threw it away. The snake vomited blood and became unconscious. It was stunned. It could not move. So, thinking it dead, the boys went their way.

"Late at night the snake regained consciousness. Slowly and with great difficulty it dragged itself into its hole; its bones were broken and it could scarcely move. Many days passed. The snake became a mere skeleton covered with a skin. Now and then, at night, it would come out in search of food. For fear of the boys it would not leave its hole during the day-time. Since receiving the sacred word from the teacher, it had given up doing harm to others. It maintained its life on dirt, leaves, or the fruit that dropped from the trees.

"About a year later the brahmachāri came that way again and asked after the snake. The cowherd boys told him that it was dead. But he couldn't believe them. He knew that the snake would not die before attaining the fruit of the holy word with which it had been initiated. He found his way to the place and, searching here and there, called it by the name he had given it. Hearing the teacher's voice, it came out of its hole and bowed before him with great reverence. 'How are you?' asked the brahmachāri.

'I am well, sir', replied the snake. 'But', the teacher asked, 'why are you so thin?' The snake replied: 'Revered sir, you ordered me not to harm anybody. So I have been living only on leaves and fruit. Perhaps that has made me thinner.'

"The snake had developed the quality of sattva; it could not be angry with anyone. It had totally forgotten that the cowherd boys had almost killed it.

"The brahmachāri said: 'It can't be mere want of food that has reduced you to this state. There must be some other reason. Think a little.' Then the snake remembered that the boys had dashed it against the ground. It said: 'Yes, revered sir, now I remember. The boys one day dashed me violently against the ground. They are ignorant, after all. They didn't realize what a great change had come over my mind. How could they know I wouldn't bite or harm anyone?' The brahmachāri exclaimed: 'What a shame! You are such a fool! You don't know how to protect yourself. I asked you not to bite, but I didn't forbid you to hiss. Why didn't you scare them by hissing?'

"So you must hiss at wicked people. You must frighten them lest they should do you harm. But never inject your venom into them. One must not injure others.

"In this creation of God there is a variety of things: men, animals, trees, plants. Among the animals some are good, some bad. There are ferocious animals like the tiger. Some trees bear fruit sweet as nectar, and others bear fruit that is poisonous. Likewise, among human beings, there are the good and the wicked, the holy and the unholy. There are some who are devoted to God, and others who are attached to the world."

"What is knowledge? And what is the nature of this ego? 'God alone is the Doer, and none else' – that is knowledge. I am not the doer; I am a mere instrument in His hand. Therefore I say: 'O Mother, Thou art the Operator and I am the machine. Thou art the Indweller and I am the house. Thou art the Driver and I am the carriage. I move as Thou movest me. I do as Thou makest me do. I speak as Thou makest me speak. Not I, not I, but Thou, but Thou.'"

"Man cannot really help the world. God alone does that – He who has created the sun and the moon, who has put love for their children in parents' hearts, endowed noble souls with compassion, and holy men and devotees with divine love. The man who works for others, without any selfish motive, really does good to himself."

"Bhakti is the one essential thing. To be sure, God exists in all beings. Who, then, is a devotee? He whose mind dwells on God. But this is not possible as long as one has egotism and vanity. The water of God's grace cannot collect on the high mound of egotism. It runs down. I am a mere machine."

"He who is called Brahman by the jnānis is known as Ātman by the yogis and as Bhagavān by the bhaktas. The same brāhmin is called priest, when worshipping in the temple, and cook, when preparing a meal in the kitchen. The jnāni, sticking to the path of knowledge, always reasons about the Reality, saying, 'Not this, not this'. Brahman is neither 'this' nor 'that'; It is neither the universe nor its living beings. Reasoning in this way, the mind becomes steady. Then it disappears and the aspirant goes into samādhi. This is the Knowledge of Brahman. It is the unwavering conviction of the jnāni that Brahman alone is real and the world illusory. All these names and forms are illusory, like a dream. What Brahman is cannot be described. One cannot even say that Brahman is a Person. This is the opinion of the jnānis, the followers of Vedānta philosophy."

"The Primordial Power is ever at play. She is creating, preserving, and destroying in play, as it were. This Power is called Kāli. Kāli is verily Brahman, and Brahman is verily Kāli. It is one and the same Reality. When we think of It as inactive, that is to say, not engaged in the acts of creation, preservation, and destruction, then we call It Brahman. But when It engages in these activities, then we call It Kāli or Śakti. The Reality is one and the same; the difference is in name and form."

"A man verily becomes liberated in life if he feels: 'God is the Doer. He alone is doing everything. I am doing nothing.' Man's sufferings and worries spring only from his persistent thought that he is the doer."

Master (*to the devotees*): "A man becomes liberated even in this life when he knows that God is the Doer of all things. Once Keshab came here with Sambhu Mallick. I said to him, 'Not even a leaf moves except by the will of God.' Where is man's free will? All are under the will of God. Nangtā was a man of great knowledge, yet even he was about to drown himself in the Ganges. He stayed here eleven months. At one time he suffered from stomach trouble. The excruciating pain made him lose control over himself, and he wanted to drown himself in the river. There was a long shoal near the bathing-ghāt. However far he went into the river, he couldn't find water above his knees. Then he understood everything and came back."

"God doesn't easily appear in the heart of a man who feels himself to be his own master. But God can be seen the moment His grace descends. He is the Sun of Knowledge. One single ray of His has illumined the world with the light of knowledge. That is how we are able to see one another and acquire varied knowledge. One can see God only if He turns His light toward His own face."

"I am the machine and God is the Operator. I act as He makes me act. I speak as He makes me speak."

"Those whose spiritual consciousness has been awakened never make a false step. They do not have to reason in order to shun evil. They are so full of love of God that whatever action they undertake is a good action. They are fully conscious that they are not the doers of their actions, but mere servants of God. They always feel: 'I am the machine and He is the Operator. I do as He does through me. I speak as He speaks through me. I move as He moves me.'

"Fully awakened souls are beyond virtue and vice. They realize that it is God who does everything.

"There was a monastery in a certain place. The monks residing there went out daily to beg their food. One day a monk, while out for his alms, saw a landlord beating a man mercilessly. The compassionate monk stepped in and asked the landlord to stop. But the landlord was filled with anger and turned his wrath against the innocent monk. He beat the monk till he fell unconscious on the ground. Someone reported the matter to the monastery. The monks ran to the spot and found their brother lying there. Four or five of them carried him back and laid him on a bed. He was still unconscious. The other monks sat around him sad at heart;

some were fanning him. Finally someone suggested that he should be given a little milk to drink. When it was poured into his mouth he regained consciousness. He opened his eyes and looked around. One of the monks said, 'Let us see whether he is fully conscious and can recognize us.' Shouting into his ear, he said, 'Revered sir, who is giving you milk?' 'Brother', replied the holy man in a low voice, 'He who beat me is now giving me milk.'"

"What can you do? Be ready for Death. Death has entered the house. You must fight him with the weapon of God's holy name. God alone is the Doer. I say: 'O Lord, I do as Thou doest through me. I speak as Thou speakest through me. I am the machine and Thou art the Operator. I am the house and Thou art the Indweller. I am the engine and Thou art the Engineer.' Give your power of attorney to God. One doesn't come to grief through letting a good man assume one's responsibilities. Let His will be done."

"You are a deputy magistrate. Remember that you have obtained your position through the grace of God. Do not forget Him, but remember that all men must one day walk down the same path. We stay in the world only a couple of days."

Vaidyanath: "Sir, I have a doubt. People speak of free will. They say that a man can do either good or evil according to his will. Is it true? Are we really free to do whatever we like?"

Master: "Everything depends on the will of God. The world is His play. He has created all these different things – great and small, strong and weak, good and bad, virtuous and vicious. This is all His māyā, His sport. You must have observed that all the trees in a garden are not of the same kind.

"As long as a man has not realized God, he thinks he is free. It is God Himself who keeps this error in man. Otherwise sin would have multiplied. Man would not have been afraid of sin, and there would have been no punishment for it.

"But do you know the attitude of one who has realized God? He feels: 'I am the machine, and Thou, O Lord, art the Operator. I am the house and Thou art the Indweller. I am the chariot and Thou art the Driver. I move as Thou movest me; I speak as Thou makest me speak.'"

"Direct the six passions to God. The impulse of *lust* should be turned into the desire to have intercourse with Ātman. Feel *angry* at those who stand in your way to God. Feel *greedy* for Him. If you must have the feeling of *I and mine*, then associate it with God. Say, for instance, 'My Rāma, my Krishna.' If you must have *pride*, then feel like Bibhishana, who said, 'I have touched the feet of Rāma with my head; I will not bow this head before anyone else.'"

"If a man has the firm conviction that God alone is the Doer and he is His instrument, then he cannot do anything sinful."

"Both worldliness and liberation depend on God's will. It is God alone who has kept man in the world in a state of ignorance; and man will be free when God, of His own sweet will, calls him to Himself. It is like the mother calling the child at meal-time, when he is out playing. When the time comes for setting a man free, God makes him seek the company of holy men. Further, it is God who makes him restless for spiritual life."

"A man who has realized God shows certain character-istics... Further, he is firmly convinced that he is the machine and God is its Operator, that God alone is the Doer and all others are His instruments. As some Śikh devotees once said to me, even the leaf moves because of God's will. One should be aware that everything happens by the will of Rāma."

"Knowledge makes one feel: 'O God, Thou art the Doer and I am Thy instrument. O God, to Thee belongs all – body, mind, house, family, living beings, and the universe. All these are Thine. Nothing belongs to me.'"

"Once I talked to Keshab Sen about the Knowledge of Brahman. He asked me to explain it further. I said, 'If I proceed further, then you won't be able to preserve your organization and following.' 'Then please stop here!' replied Keshab. (*All laugh.*) But still I said to Keshab: '"I" and "mine" indicate ignorance. Without ignorance one cannot have such a feeling as "I am the doer; these are my wife, children, possessions, name and fame".' Thereupon Keshab said, 'Sir, if one gave up the "I", nothing whatsoever would remain.' I reassured him and said: 'I am not asking you to give up all of the "I". You should give up only the "unripe I". The "unripe I" makes one feel: "I am the doer. These are my wife and children. I am a teacher." Renounce this, "unripe I" and keep the "ripe I", which will make you feel that you are the servant of God, His devotee, and that God is the Doer and you are His instrument.'"

"One day I had the vision of Consciousness, non-dual and indivisible. At first it had been revealed to me that there were innumerable men, animals, and other creatures. Among them there were aristocrats, the English, the Mussalmāns, myself, scavengers, dogs, and also a bearded Mussalmān with an earthenware tray of rice in his hand. He put a few grains of rice into everybody's mouth. I too tasted a little.

"Another day I saw rice, vegetables, and other food-stuff, and filth and dirt as well, lying around. Suddenly the soul came out of my body and, like a flame, touched everything. It was like a protruding tongue of fire and tasted everything once, even the excreta. It was revealed to me that all these are one Substance, the non-dual and indivisible Consciousness."

"A guru said to his disciple, 'It is Rāma alone who resides in all bodies.' The disciple was a man of great faith. One day a dog snatched a piece of bread from him and started to run away. He ran after the dog, with a jar of butter in his hand, and cried again and again: 'O Rāma, stand still a minute. That bread hasn't been buttered.'"

"Sometimes I too feel that way. The Mother reveals to me that She Herself has become everything. One day I was coming from the pine-grove toward the Panchavati. A dog followed me. I stood still for a while near the Panchavati. The thought came to my mind that the Mother might say something to me through that dog."

"As long as you do not feel that God is the Master, you must come back to the world, you must be born again and again. There will be no rebirth when you can truly say, 'O God, Thou art the Master.' As long as you cannot say, 'O Lord, Thou alone art real', you will not be released from the life of the world. This going and coming, this rebirth, is inevitable. There will be no liberation. Further, what can you achieve by saying, 'It is mine'? The manager of an estate may say, 'This is our garden; these are our couches and furniture.' But when he is dismissed by the master, he hasn't the right to take away even a chest of worthless mango-wood given to him for his use.

"The feeling of 'I and mine' has covered the Reality. Because of this we do not see Truth. Attainment of Chaitanya, Divine Consciousness, is not possible without the knowledge of Advaita, Non-duality. After realizing Chaitanya one enjoys Nityānanda, Eternal Bliss. One enjoys this Bliss after attaining the state of a paramahamsa."

Ishan: "It is mentioned in a hymn in the *Chandi* that Brahman alone is the Primal Energy. Brahman is identical with Śakti."

Master: "It will not do simply to express that idea in words. Only when you assimilate it will all be well with you.

"When the heart becomes pure through the practice of spiritual discipline, then one rightly feels that God alone is the Doer. He alone has become mind, life, and intelligence. We are only His instruments."

"All doubts disappear after the realization of God. Then the devotee meets the favourable wind. He becomes free from worry. He is like the boatman who, when the favourable wind blows, unfurls the sail, holds the rudder lightly, and enjoys a smoke."

"As long as a man associates himself with upādhis, so long he sees the manifold, such as Keshab, Prasanna, Amrita, and so on; but on attaining Perfect Knowledge he sees only one Consciousness everywhere. The same Perfect Knowledge, again, makes him realize that the one Consciousness has become the universe and its living beings and the twenty-four cosmic principles. But the manifestations of Divine Power are different in different beings. It is He, undoubtedly, who has become everything; but in some cases there is a greater manifestation than in others."

"Give God the power of attorney. Let Him do whatever He wants. I am the machine and God is its Operator."

"When it (mind) becomes pure, one has another experience. One realizes: 'God alone is the Doer, and I am His instrument.' One does not feel oneself to be absolutely necessary to others either in their misery or in their happiness."

"Referring to a certain place, someone once said to me: 'Nobody sings the name of God there. It has no holy atmosphere.' No sooner did he say this than I perceived that it was God alone who had become all living beings. They appeared as countless bubbles, or reflections in the Ocean of Satchidānanda.

"Again, I find sometimes that living beings are like so many pills made of Indivisible Consciousness. Once I was on my way to Burdwan from Kāmārpukur. At one place I ran to the meadow to see how living beings are sustained. I saw ants crawling there. It appeared to me that every place was filled with Consciousness."

Hazra entered the room and sat on the floor.

Master: "Again, I perceive that living beings are like different flowers with various layers of petals. They are also revealed to me as bubbles, some big, some small."

While describing in this way the vision of different divine forms, the Master went into an ecstatic state and said, "I have become! I am here!" Uttering these words he went into samādhi. His body was motionless. He remained in that state a long time and then gradually regained partial consciousness of the world. He began to laugh like a boy and pace the room. His eyes radiated bliss as if he had seen a wondrous vision. His gaze was not fixed on any particular object, and his face beamed with joy. Still pacing the room, the Master said: "I saw the paramahamsa who stayed under the banyan tree walking thus with just such a smile. Am I too in that state of mind?"

He sat on the small couch and engaged in conversation with the Divine Mother.

Master: "I don't even care to know. Mother, may I have pure love for Thy Lotus Feet!"

Master (*with a smile*): "That is true. Nothing comes to pass except at the right time. Going to bed, a child said to his mother, 'Mother, please wake me up when I feel the call of nature.' 'My son', said the mother, 'that urge itself will wake you up. I don't have to wake you.'"

"It is all decided beforehand by God what each one shall receive."

Musician: "It is God alone who is both the 'instrument' and the 'cause'. Duryodhana said to Krishna: 'O Lord, Thou art seated in my heart. I act as Thou makest me act.'"

Master (*with a smile*): "Yes, that is true. It is God alone who acts through us. He is the Doer, undoubtedly, and man is His instrument. But it is also true that an action cannot fail to produce its result. Your stomach will certainly burn if you eat hot chilli. It is God who has ordained that chilli will burn your stomach."

"When you realize God, will you pray to Him, 'O God, please grant that I may dig reservoirs, build roads, and found hospitals and dispensaries'? After the realization of God all such desires are left behind.

"Then mustn't one perform acts of compassion, such as charity to the poor? I do not forbid it. If a man has money, he should give it to remove the sorrows and sufferings that come to his notice. In such an event the wise man says, 'Give the poor something.' But inwardly he feels: 'What can I do? God alone is the Doer. I am nothing.'"

"It is God alone who does everything. You may say that in that case man may commit sin. But that is not true. If a man is firmly convinced that God alone is the Doer and that he himself is nothing, then he will never make a false step.

"It is God alone who has planted in man's mind what the 'Englishman' calls free will. People who have not realized God would become engaged in more and more sinful actions if God had not planted in them the notion of free will. Sin would have increased if God had not made the sinner feel that he alone was responsible for his sin."

"Those who have realized God are aware that free will is a mere appearance. In reality man is the machine and God its Operator, man is the carriage and God its Driver."

Master (*smiling*): "What will a man gain by knowing many scriptures? The one thing needful is to know how to cross the river of the world. God alone is real, and all else illusory.

"While Arjuna was aiming his arrow at the eye of the bird, Drona asked him: 'What do you see? Do you see these kings?' 'No, sir', replied Arjuna. 'Do you see me?' 'No.' 'The tree?' 'No.' 'The bird on the tree?' 'No.' 'What do you see then?' 'Only the eye of the bird.'

"He who sees only the eye of the bird can hit the mark. He alone is clever who sees that God is real and all else is illusory."

"There are three classes of devotees. The lowest one says, 'God is up there.' That is, he points to heaven. The mediocre devotee says that God dwells in the heart as the 'Inner Controller'. But the highest devotee says: 'God alone has become everything. All that we perceive is so many forms of God.' Narendra used to make fun of me and say: 'Yes, God has become all! Then a pot is God, a cup is God!' (*Laughter.*)

"All doubts disappear when one sees God. It is one thing to hear of God, but quite a different thing to see Him. A man cannot have one hundred per cent conviction through mere hearing. But if he beholds God face to face, then he is wholly convinced.

"Formal worship drops away after the vision of God. It was thus that my worship in the temple came to an end. I used to worship the Deity in the Kāli temple. It was suddenly revealed to me that everything is Pure Spirit. The utensils of worship, the altar, the door-frame – all Pure Spirit. Men, animals, and other living beings – all Pure Spirit. Then like a madman I began to shower flowers in all directions. Whatever I saw I worshipped."

"The feeling 'I am the doer' is the outcome of ignorance. But the feeling that God does everything is due to knowledge. God alone is the Doer; all others are mere instruments in His hands."

"Sambhu Mallick once said to me, 'Please bless me, sir, that I may spend all my money for good purposes, such as building hospitals and dispensaries, making roads, and digging wells.' I said to him: 'It will be good if you can do these things in a spirit of detachment. But that is very difficult. Whatever you may do, you must always remember that the aim of this life of yours is the attainment of God and not the building of hospitals and dispensaries. Suppose God appeared before you and said to you, "Accept a boon from Me." Would you then ask Him, "O God, build me some hospitals and dispensaries"? Or would you not rather pray to Him: "O God, may I have pure love at Your Lotus Feet! May I have Your uninterrupted vision!"? Hospitals, dispensaries, and all such things are unreal. God alone is real and all else unreal. Furthermore, after realizing God one feels that He alone is the Doer and we are but His instruments. Then why should we forget Him and destroy ourselves by being involved in too many activities? After realizing Him, one may, through His grace, become His instrument in building many hospitals and dispensaries.'"

"This feeling, 'I am the doer', is ignorance. On the contrary, the idea, 'O God, Thou art the Doer and I am only an instrument; Thou art the Operator and I am the machine', is Knowledge. After attaining Knowledge a man says: 'O God, nothing belongs to me – neither this house of worship nor this Kālī temple nor this Brāhmo Samāj. These are all Thine. Wife, son, and family do not belong to me. They are all Thine.'

"To love these objects, regarding them as one's own, is māyā. But to love all things is dayā, compassion. To love only the members of the Brāhmo Samāj or of one's own family is māyā; to love one's own countrymen is māyā. But to love the people of all countries, to love the members of all religions, is dayā. Such love comes from love of God, from dayā."

"The idea of responsibility! Goodness gracious! Men like Śankarāchārya and Śukadeva kept the 'ego of Knowledge'. It is not for man to show compassion, but for God. One feels compassion as long as one has the 'ego of Knowledge'. And it is God Himself who has become the 'ego of Knowledge'.

"You may feel a thousand times that it is all magic; but you are still under the control of the Divine Mother. You cannot escape Her. You are not free. You must do what She makes you do. A man attains Brahmajnāna only when it is given to him by the Ādyāśakti, the Divine Mother. Then alone does he see the whole thing as magic; otherwise not."

"He is indeed a real man who has harmonized everything. Most people are one-sided. But I find that all opinions point to the One. All views – the Sākta, the Vaishnava, the Vedānta – have that One for their centre. He who is formless is, again, endowed with form. It is He who appears in different forms. 'The attributeless Brahman is my Father. God with attributes is my Mother. Whom shall I blame? Whom shall I praise? The two pans of the scales are equally heavy.'"

Sri Ramakrishna returned to his room and sat on the small couch. He began to praise a medicine that a certain brahmachāri had prepared for him. Referring to this man, Hazra said: "He is now entangled in many worldly anxieties. What a shame! Look at Nabai Chaitanya of Konnagar. Though a householder, he has put on a red cloth."

Master: "What shall I say? I clearly see that it is God Himself who has assumed all these human forms. Therefore I cannot take anybody to task."

"Once upon a time a sādhu acquired great occult powers. He was vain about them. But he was a good man and had some austerities to his credit. One day the Lord, disguised as a holy man, came to him and said, 'Revered sir, I have heard that you have great occult powers.' The sādhu received the Lord cordially and offered him a seat. Just then an elephant passed by. The Lord, in the disguise of the holy man, said to the sādhu, 'Revered sir, can you kill this elephant if you like?' The sādhu said, 'Yes, it is possible.' So saying, he took a pinch of dust, muttered some mantras over it, and threw it at the elephant. The beast struggled awhile in pain and then dropped dead. The Lord said: 'What power you have! You have killed the elephant!' The sādhu laughed. Again the Lord spoke: 'Now can you revive the elephant?' 'That too is possible', replied the sādhu. He threw another pinch of charmed dust at the beast. The elephant writhed about a little and came back to life. Then the Lord said: 'Wonderful is your power. But may I ask you one thing? You have killed the elephant and you have revived it. But what has that done for you? Do you feel uplifted by it? Has it enabled you to realize God?' Saying this, the Lord vanished."

"The Lord said to Prahlāda, 'Ask a boon of Me.' 'I have seen You', replied Prahlāda. 'That is enough. I don't need anything else.' But the Lord insisted. Thereupon Prahlāda said, 'If You must give me a boon, let it be that those who have tortured me may not have to suffer punishment.' The meaning of those words is that it was God who tortured Prahlāda in the form of his persecutors, and, if they suffered punishment, it would really be God who suffered."

Master (*to Vijay, with a smile*): "I was told that you had put up a 'signboard' here that people belonging to other faiths are not allowed to come in. Narendra, too, said to me: 'You shouldn't go to the Brāhmo Samāj. You had better visit Shivanath's house.'

"But I say that we are all calling on the same God. Jealousy and malice need not be. Some say that God is formless, and some that God has form. I say, let one man meditate on God with form if he believes in form, and let another meditate on the formless Deity if he does not believe in form. What I mean is that dogmatism is not good. It is not good to feel that my religion alone is true and other religions are false. The correct attitude is this: My religion is right, but I do not know whether other religions are right or wrong, true or false. I say this because one cannot know the true nature of God unless one realizes Him. Kabir used to say: 'God with form is my Mother, the Formless is my Father. Which shall I blame? Which shall I praise? The two pans of the scales are equally heavy.'

"Hindus, Mussalmāns, Christians, Sāktas, Saivas, Vaishnavas, the Brahmajnānis of the time of the rishis,

70

and you, the Brahmajnānis of modern times, all seek the same object. A mother prepares dishes to suit the stomachs of her children. Suppose a mother has five children and a fish is bought for the family. She doesn't cook pilau or kāliā for all of them. All have not the same power of digestion; so she prepares a simple stew for some. But she loves all her children equally."

Surendra stood near Sri Ramakrishna. He was in the habit of drinking and often went to excess. This had worried the Master greatly, but he had not asked Surendra to give up drinking altogether. He had said to him: "Look here, Surendra! Whenever you drink wine, offer it beforehand to the Divine Mother. See that your brain doesn't become clouded and that you don't reel. The more you think of the Divine Mother, the less you will like to drink. The Mother is the Giver of the bliss of divine inebriation. Realizing Her, one feels a natural bliss."

The Master looked at Surendra and said, "You have had a drink." With these words he went into samādhi.

"When a man has true knowledge he feels that everything is filled with Consciousness."

Kedar: "God assumes forms for the sake of His devotees. Through ecstatic love a devotee sees God with form. Dhruva had a vision of the Lord. He said: 'Why don't your ear-rings move?' The Lord said, 'They will move if you move them.'"

Master: "One must accept everything: God with form and God without form. While meditating in the Kāli temple I noticed Ramani, a prostitute. I said, 'Mother, I see that Thou art in that form too.' Therefore I say one must accept everything. One does not know when or how God will reveal Himself."

"I said to Hazra, 'Don't speak ill of anyone.' It is Nārāyana Himself who has assumed all these forms."

"'I' and 'mine' – that is ignorance. True knowledge makes one feel: 'O God, You alone do everything. You alone are my own. And to You alone belong houses, buildings, family, relatives, friends, the whole world. All is Yours.' But ignorance makes one feel: 'I am doing everything. I am the doer. House, buildings, family, children, friends, and property are all mine.'"

"I am the machine and She is the Operator. I am the house and She is the Indweller. I am the chariot and She is the Charioteer. I move as She moves me; I speak as She speaks through me. In the Kaliyuga one does not hear the voice of God, it is said, except through the mouth of a child or a madman or some such person.

"A man cannot be a guru. Everything happens by the will of God. Heinous sins – the sins of many births – and accumulated ignorance all disappear in the twinkling of an eye, through the grace of God. When light enters a room that has been kept dark a thousand years, does it remove the thousand years' darkness little by little, or instantly? Of course, at the mere touch of light all the darkness disappears.

"What can a man do? He may speak many words, but after all is said and done everything rests with God. The lawyer says: 'I have said all that can be said. Now the verdict rests with the judge.'"

"Now, whom should we call the siddha? He who has the absolute conviction that God exists and is the sole Doer; he who has seen God."

"When one has Knowledge one does not see God any more at a distance. One does not think of Him any more as 'He'. He becomes 'This'. Then He is seen in one's own heart. God dwells in every man."

"Three words – 'master', 'teacher', and 'father' – prick me like thorns. I am the son of God, His eternal child. How can I be a 'father'? God alone is the Master and I am His instrument. He is the Operator and I am the machine."

"In a certain village there lived a weaver. He was a very pious soul. Everyone trusted him and loved him. He used to sell his goods in the market-place. When a customer asked him the price of a piece of cloth, the weaver would say: 'By the will of Rāma the price of the yarn is one rupee and the labour four ānnās; by the will of Rāma the profit is two ānnās. The price of the cloth, by the will of Rāma, is one rupee and six ānnās.' Such was the people's faith in the weaver that the customer would at once pay the price and take the cloth. The weaver was a real devotee of God. After finishing his supper in the evening, he would spend long hours in the worship hall meditating on God and chanting His name and glories. Now, late one night the weaver couldn't get to sleep. He was sitting in the worship hall, smoking now and then, when a band of robbers happened to pass that way. They wanted a man to carry their goods and said to the weaver, 'Come with us.' So saying, they led him off by the hand. After committing a robbery in a house, they put a load of things on the weaver's head, commanding him to carry them. Suddenly the police arrived and the robbers ran away. But the weaver, with his load, was arrested. He was kept in the lock-up for the night. Next day he was brought before the magistrate for trial. The villagers learnt what had happened and came to court. They said to the magistrate, 'Your Honour, this man could never commit a robbery.' Thereupon the magistrate asked the weaver to make his statement.

"The weaver said: 'Your Honour, by the will of Rāma I finished my meal at night. Then by the will of Rāma I was sitting in the worship hall. It was quite late at night by the will of Rāma. By the will of Rāma I had been thinking of God and chanting His name and glories, when by the will of Rāma a band of robbers passed that way. By the will of Rāma they dragged me with them; by the will of Rāma they committed a robbery in a house; and by the will of Rāma they put a load on my head. Just then, by the will of Rāma the police arrived, and by the will of Rāma I was arrested. Then by the will of Rāma the police kept me in the lock-up for the night, and this morning by the will of Rāma I have been brought before Your Honour.' The magistrate realized that the weaver was a pious man and ordered his release. On his way home the weaver said to his friends, 'By the will of Rāma I have been released.'

"Whether a man should be a householder or a monk depends on the will of Rāma. Surrender everything to God and do your duties in the world. What else can you do? A clerk was once sent to prison. After the prison term was over he was released. Now, what do you think he did? Cut capers or do his old clerical work?"

"He who has seen God knows truly that God alone is the Doer, that it is He who does everything."

Quoting from the *Gitā*, Bhavani said: "He who sees Me in all things and all things in Me, never becomes separated from Me, nor do I become separated from him. That yogi who, established in unity, worships Me dwelling in all beings, abides in Me, whatever his mode of life. O Arjuna, that yogi is regarded as the highest who judges the pleasure and pain of all beings by the same standard that he applies to himself."

Master: "These are the characteristics of the highest bhakta."

"'A little shopkeeping is necessary'! One speaks as one thinks. If a man thinks of worldly things day and night, and deals with people hypocritically, then his words are coloured by his thoughts. If one eats radish, one belches radish. Instead of talking about 'shopkeeping', he should rather have said, 'A man should act as if he were the doer, knowing very well that he is really not the doer.' The other day a man was singing here. The song contained words like 'profit' and 'loss'. I stopped him. If one contemplates a particular subject day and night, one cannot talk of anything else."

"Everything happens by the will of God. If your spiritual consciousness has been awakened at this place, know that I am only an instrument. 'Uncle Moon is everybody's uncle.' All happens by the will of God."

Three or four devotees stood near Sri Ramakrishna on the verandah and listened to his words about the exalted state of the paramahamsa. The Master said: "A paramahamsa is always conscious that God alone is real and all else illusory. Only the swan has the power to separate milk from a mixture of milk and water. The swan's tongue secretes an acid that separates the milk from the mixture. The paramahamsa also possesses such a juice; it is his ecstatic love for God. That separates the Real from the mixture of the Real and the unreal. Through it one becomes aware of God and sees Him."

Master: "Don't misunderstand me. (*To Narendra*) You say
you understand people; that is why I am telling you all this.
Do you know how I look on people like Hazra? I know
that just as God takes the form of holy men, so He also
takes the form of cheats and rogues. (*To Mahimacharan*)
What do you say? All are God."

Mahima: "Yes, sir. All are God."

"Is it an easy thing to obtain the Knowledge of Brahman?
It is not possible unless the mind is annihilated."

"With the annihilation of the mind dies the ego, which says 'I', 'I'."

"To tell you the truth, everything happens by God's will. When He says 'Yea', everything comes to pass, and when He says 'Nay', everything comes to a standstill.

"Why is it that one man should not bless another? Because nothing can happen by man's will: things come to pass or disappear by God's will."

"It is God who does everything. We are His instruments. Some Śikhs said to me in front of the Kālī temple, 'God is compassionate.' I said, 'To whom is He compassionate?' 'Why, revered sir, to all of us', said the Śikhs. I said: 'We are His children. Does compassion to one's own children mean much? A father must look after his children; or do you expect the people of the neighbourhood to bring them up?' Well, won't those who say that God is compassionate ever understand that we are God's children and not someone else's?"

"Just try to find out who this 'I' is. While you are searching for 'I', 'He' comes out. 'I am the machine and He is the Operator.' You have heard of a mechanical toy that goes into a store with a letter in its hand. You are like that toy. God alone is the Doer. Do your duties in the world as if you were the doer, but knowing all the time that God alone is the Doer and you are the instrument."

"Try to find out what this 'I' is. Is this 'I' the bones or flesh or blood or intestines? Seeking the 'I', you discover 'Thou'. In other words, nothing exists inside you but the power of God. There is no 'I', but only 'He'. (*To Pasupati*) You have so much wealth, but you have no egotism. It is not possible to rid oneself altogether of the ego; so, as long as it is there, let the rascal remain as the servant of God."

Master (*to Nanda*): "According to the *Gitā* a man who is honoured and respected by many people possesses a special power of God. You have divine power."

Nanda: "All men have the same power."

Master (*sharply*): "You all say the same thing. Can all men ever possess power to the same degree? God no doubt dwells in all beings as the all-pervading Spirit, but the manifestations of His Power are different in different beings.

"Vidyāsagār, too, said the same thing. He said, 'Has God given some more power and some less?' Thereupon I said to him: 'If there are not different manifestations of His Power, then why have we come to see you? Have you grown two horns on your head?'"

"You have a very fine nature. There are two characteristics of knowledge: a peaceful nature and absence of pride."

"If this ego cannot be got rid of, then let the rascal remain as the servant of God. (*All laugh.*)

"A man may keep this ego even after attaining samādhi. Such a man feels either that he is a servant of God or that he is a lover of God. Śankarāchārya retained the 'ego of Knowledge' to teach men spiritual life. The 'servant-ego', the 'Knowledge ego', or the 'devotee ego' may be called the 'ripe ego'. It is different from the 'unripe ego', which makes one feel: 'I am the doer. I am the son of a wealthy man. I am learned. I am rich. How dare anyone slight me?' A man with an 'unripe ego' cherishes such ideas. Suppose a thief has entered such a man's house and stolen some of his belongings. If the thief is caught, all the articles will be snatched away from him. Then he will be beaten. At last he will be handed over to the police. The owner of the stolen goods will say: 'What! This rogue doesn't know whose house he has entered!'

"After realizing God, a man becomes like a child five years old. The ego of such a man may be called the 'ego of a child', the 'ripe ego'. The child is not under the control of any of the gunas. He is beyond the three gunas. He is not under the control of any of the gunas – sattva, rajas, or tamas. Just watch a child and you will find that he is not under the influence of tamas. One moment he quarrels with his chum or even fights with him, and the next moment he hugs him, shows him much affection, and plays with him again. He is not even under the control of rajas. Now he builds his play house and makes all kinds of plans to make it beautiful, and the next moment he leaves everything behind and runs to his mother. Again, you see him wearing a beautiful piece of cloth worth five rupees. After a few moments the cloth lies on the ground; he forgets all about it. Or he may carry it under his arm. If you say to the child: 'That's a beautiful piece of cloth. Whose is it?', he answers: 'Why, it is mine. My daddy gave it to me.' You may say, 'My darling, won't you give it to me?' and he will reply: 'Oh no, it is mine. My daddy gave it to me. I won't give it to you.' Some minutes later you may coax him with a toy or a music-box worth a penny, and he will give you the cloth. Again, a child five years old is not attached even to sattva. You may find him today very fond of his playmates in the neighbourhood; he doesn't feel happy for a moment without seeing them; but tomorrow, when he goes to another place with his parents, he finds new playmates; all his love is now directed to his new friends, and he almost forgets about his old ones. Further, a child has no pride of caste or family. If his mother says to him about a certain person, 'This man is your elder brother', he believes this to be one hundred per cent true. One of the two may have been born in a brāhmin family and the other may belong to a low caste, say that of the blacksmiths, but they will take their meal from the same plate. A child is beyond all ideas of purity and impurity.

He is not bound by social conventions. He doesn't hesitate to come out naked before others.

"Then there is an 'ego of old age'. (*Dr. Sarkar laughs.*) An old man has many shackles: caste, pride, shame, hatred, and fear. Furthermore, he is bound by the ideas of worldly cleverness, calculating intelligence, and deceit. If he is angry with anybody, he cannot shake it off easily; perhaps he keeps the feeling as long as he lives. Again, there is the 'ego of scholarship' and the 'ego of wealth'. The 'ego of old age' is an 'unripe ego'.

(*To the doctor*) "There are a few men who cannot attain knowledge of God: men proud of their scholarship, proud of their education, or proud of their wealth. If you speak to such people about a holy man and ask them to visit him, they make all kinds of excuses and will not go. But in their heart of hearts they think: 'Why, we are big people ourselves. Must we go and visit someone else?'

"A characteristic of tamas is pride. Pride and delusion come from tamas.

"It is said in the Purāna that Rāvana had an excess of rajas, Kumbhakarna of tamas, and Bibhishana of sattva. That is why Bibhishana was able to receive the grace of Rāma. Another characteristic of tamas is anger. Through anger one loses one's wits and cannot distinguish between right and wrong. In a fit of anger Hanuman set fire to Lankā, without thinking for a moment that the fire might also burn down the hut where Sitā lived.

"Still another feature of tamas is lust. Girindra Ghosh of Pāthuriāghāta once remarked, 'Since you cannot get rid of your passions – your lust, your anger, and so on – give them a new direction. Instead of desiring worldly pleasures, desire God. Have intercourse with Brahman. If you cannot get rid of anger, then change its direction. Assume the tamasic attitude of bhakti, and say: 'What? I have repeated the hallowed name of Durgā, and shall I not be liberated? How can I be a sinner anymore? How can I be bound anymore?' If you cannot get rid of temptation, direct it toward God. Be infatuated with God's beauty. If you cannot get rid of pride, then be proud to say that you are the servant of God, you are the child of God. Thus turn the six passions toward God."

"You know I am a fool. I know nothing. Then who is it that says all these things? I say to the Divine Mother: 'O Mother, I am the machine and Thou art the Operator. I am the house and Thou art the Indweller. I am the chariot and Thou art the Charioteer. I do as Thou makest me do; I speak as Thou makest me speak; I move as Thou makest me move. It is not I! It is not I! It is all Thou! It is all Thou!' Hers is the glory; we are only Her instruments. Once Rādhā, to prove her chastity, carried on her head a pitcher filled with water. The pitcher had a thousand holes, but not a drop of water spilled. People began to praise her, saying, 'Such a chaste woman the world will never see again!' Then Rādhā said to them: 'Why do you praise me? Say: Glory unto Krishna! Hail Krishna! I am only His handmaid.'"

"Once I said to Mathur Babu: 'Don't think that I have achieved my desired end because you, a rich man, show me respect. It matters very little to me whether you obey me or not.' Of course you must remember that a mere man can do nothing. It is God alone who makes one person obey another. Man is straw and dust before the power of God."

Doctor: "Do you think I shall obey you because a certain fisherman obeyed you? ... Undoubtedly I show you respect; I show you respect as a man."

Master: "Do I ask you to show me respect?"

Girish: "Does he ask you to show him respect?"

Doctor (*to the Master*): "What are you saying? Do you explain it as the will of God?"

Master: "What else can it be? What can a man do before the will of God? Arjuna said to Sri Krishna on the battlefield of Kurukshetra: 'I will not fight. It is impossible for me to kill my own kinsmen.' Sri Krishna replied: 'Arjuna, you will have to fight. Your very nature will make you fight.' Then Sri Krishna revealed to Arjuna that all the men on the battlefield were already dead.

"Once some Śikhs came to the Kāli temple at Dakshine-swar. They said: 'You see, the leaves of the aśwattha tree are moving. That too is due to the will of God.' Without His will not even a leaf can move."

Doctor: "If everything is done by the will of God, then why do you chatter? Why do you talk so much to bring knowledge to others?"

Master: "He makes me talk; therefore I talk. 'I am the machine and He is the Operator.'"

Doctor: "You say that you are the machine. That's all right. Or keep quiet, knowing that everything is God."

Girish (to the doctor): "Whatever you may think, sir, the truth is that we act because He makes us act. Can anyone take a single step against the Almighty Will?"

Doctor: "But God has also given us free will. I can think of God, or not, as I like."

Girish: "You think of God or do some good work because you like to. Really it is not you who do these things, but your liking of them that makes you do so."

Doctor: "Why should that be so? I do these things as my duty."

Girish: "Even then it is because you like to do your duty."

Doctor: "Suppose a child is being burnt. From a sense of duty I rush to save it."

Girish: "You feel happy to save the child; therefore you rush into the fire. It is your happiness that drives you to the action. A man eats opium being tempted by such relishes as puffed rice or fried potatoes." (Laughter)

Master: "A man must have some kind of faith before he undertakes a work. Further, he feels joy when he thinks of it. Only then does he set about performing the work. Suppose a jar of gold coins is hidden underground. First of all a man must have faith that the jar of gold coins is there. He feels joy at the thought of the jar. Then he begins to dig. As he removes the earth he hears a metallic sound. That increases his joy. Next he sees a corner of the jar. That gives him more joy. Thus his joy is ever on the increase. Standing on the porch of the Kāli temple, I have watched the ascetics preparing their smoke of hemp. I have seen their faces beaming with joy in anticipation of the smoke."

Doctor: "But take the case of fire. It gives both heat and light. The light no doubt illumines objects, but the heat burns the body. Likewise, it is not an unadulterated joy that one reaps from the performance of duty. Duty has its painful side too."

M. (to Girish): "As the proverb goes: 'If the stomach gets food, then the back can bear a few blows from the host.' There is joy in sorrow also."

Girish (to the doctor): "Duty is dry."

Doctor: "Why so?"

Girish: "Then it is pleasant." (All laugh.)

M: "Again we come to the point that one likes opium for the sake of the relishes that are served with it."

Girish (to the doctor): "Duty must be pleasant; or why do you perform it?"

Doctor: "The mind is inclined that way."

M. (to Girish): "That wretched inclination draws the mind. If you speak of the compelling power of inclination, then where is free will?"

Doctor: "I do not say that the will is absolutely free. Suppose a cow is tied with a rope. She is free within the length of that rope, but when she feels the pull of the rope—"

Master: "Jadu Mallick also gave that illustration. (*To the younger Naren*) Is it mentioned in some English book?

(*To the doctor*) "Look here. If a man truly believes that God alone does everything, that He is the Operator and man the machine, then such a man is verily liberated in life. 'Thou workest Thine own work; men only call it theirs.' Do you know what it is like? Vedanta philosophy gives an illustration. Suppose you are cooking rice in a pot, with potato, egg-plant, and other vegetables. After a while the potatoes, egg-plant, rice, and the rest begin to jump about in the pot. They seem to say with pride: 'We are moving! We are jumping!' The children see it and think the potatoes, egg-plant, and rice are alive and so they jump that way. But the elders, who know, explain to the children that the vegetables and the rice are not alive; they jump not of themselves, but because of the fire under the pot; if you remove the burning wood from the hearth, then they will move no more. Likewise the pride of man, that he is the doer, springs from ignorance. Men are powerful because of the power of God. All becomes quiet when that burning wood is taken away. The puppets dance well on the stage when pulled by a wire, but they cannot move when the wire snaps.

"A man will cherish the illusion that he is the doer as long as he has not seen God, as long as he has not touched the Philosopher's Stone. So long will he know the distinction between his good and bad actions. This awareness of distinction is due to God's māyā; and it is necessary for the purpose of running His illusory world. But a man can realize God if he takes shelter under His Vidyā-māyā and follows the path of righteousness. He who knows God and realizes Him is able to go beyond māyā. He who firmly believes that God alone is the Doer and he himself a mere instrument is a jīvanmukta, a free soul though living in a body. I said this to Keshab Chandra Sen."

Girish (*to the doctor*): "How do you know that free will exists?"

Doctor: "Not by reasoning; I feel it."

Girish: "In that case I may say that I and others feel the reverse. We feel that we are controlled by another." (*All laugh.*)

Addressing Dr. Sarkar, Sri Ramakrishna continued: "Look here. One cannot attain Knowledge unless one is free from egotism. There is a saying:

When shall I be free?
When 'I' shall cease to be.

'I' and 'mine' – that is ignorance. 'Thou' and Thine' – that is Knowledge. A true devotee says: 'O God, Thou alone art the Doer; Thou alone doest all. I am a mere instrument; I do as Thou makest me do. All these – wealth, possessions, nay, the universe itself – belong to Thee. This house and these relatives are Thine alone, not mine. I am Thy servant; mine is only the right to serve Thee according to Thy bidding.'"

"The ego that has been burnt in the fire of Knowledge cannot injure anybody. It is an ego only in name."

"I see that it is God Himself who has become the block, the executioner, and the victim for the sacrifice."

"I don't know much about what is good and what is bad. I do what God makes me do and speak what He makes me speak."

"You say that God wants everybody to lead a worldly life. But why don't you see it as God's will when your wife and children die? Why don't you see His will in poverty, when you haven't a morsel to eat?

"Māyā won't allow us to know the will of God. On account of God's māyā the unreal appears as real, and the real as unreal. The world is unreal. This moment it exists and the next it disappears. But on account of His māyā it seems to be real. It is only through His māyā that the ego seems to be the doer. Furthermore, on account of this māyā a man regards his wife and children, his brother and sister, his father and mother, his house and property, as his very own."

"Do you know what ignorance means? It is the feeling: 'This is my house; these are my relatives; I am the doer; and the household affairs go on smoothly because I manage them.' But to feel, 'I am the servant of God, His devotee, His son' – that is a good attitude."

Keshab smiled a little, and the Master continued: "Why do you write about me in your paper? You cannot make a man great by writing about him in books and magazines. If God makes a man great, then everybody knows about him even though he lives in a forest. When flowers bloom in the deep woods, the bees find them, but the flies do not. What can man do? Don't look up to him. Man is but a worm. The tongue that praises you today will abuse you tomorrow. I don't want name and fame. May I always remain the humblest of the humble and the lowliest of the lowly!"

"As long as you have to live in the world, give God the power of attorney. Make over all your responsibilities to Him; let Him do as He likes. Live in the world like a maidservant in a rich man's house. She bathes her master's children, washes them, feeds them, and takes affectionate care of them in many ways, as if they were her own children; but in her heart she knows very well that they do not belong to her. No sooner is she dismissed than all is over; she has no more relationship with the children."

BIBLIOGRAPHY

1. A 13th-century Marathi saint, poet, philosopher and yogi of the Nath tradition, Dnyaneshwar's two major works: 'Dnyaneshwari' (a commentary on the Bhagavad Gita) and 'Amrutanubhav' are highly regarded as milestones in Marathi literature.

2. An English translation from *The Genius of Dnyaneshwar – His rendering on the Geeta* by Ravin Thatte, published in 2007 by Vikas Walawalkar, Ratnagiri, Maharashtra.

3. *Mahabharata*, Chapter III-27, 28.

4. Visuddhi Magga XVI, quoted D12, Buddhism A to Z, 'no self', compiled by Ronald Epstein.

5. *Talks with Sri Ramana Maharshi*, Publisher: Sri Ramanasramam, Tiruvannamalai.

6. *Sri Sai Satcharita*, Publisher: Shri Sai Baba Sansthan, Shirdi; Mumbai.

7. *Seeking Divinity* by Dr. John S. Hislop, published in 2009 by Sri Sathya Sai Sadhana Trust, Publications Division, Prasanthi Nilayam, India.

8. *The Gospel of Sri Ramakrishna*, Originally recorded in Bengali by M., a disciple of the Master, Translated into English by Swami Nikhilananda, Sri Ramakrishna Math, Mylapore, Madras, India, p. 995.

9. *Pointers from Ramesh Balsekar* by Gautam Sachdeva, published in 2008 by Yogi Impressions Books Pvt. Ltd., Mumbai, India.

10. *The Gospel of Sri Ramakrishna, op. cit.,* pp. 1025-1026.

ACKNOWLEDGEMENTS

I would like to express deep gratitude to my spiritual teacher, Ramesh Balsekar, for shining a light on the path of non-doership.

My thanks to:

My mother Santosh, always the first one to be aware of, and give feeback on, my writings.

Devika Khanna, for her insightful suggestions on the design and layout.

Shiv Sharma, for his editorial inputs.

Gabriel Halfon, for going through the Introduction.

Natasha Gupta, for helping with the proof-reading.

Girish Jathar and Sanjay Malandkar for the layout. Reshma and the Yogi Impressions team for their hard work in running everything smoothly.

For information on Gautam Sachdeva, visit:
www.gautamsachdeva.com

The author may be contacted on email:
mails@gautamsachdeva.com

For further details, contact:
Yogi Impressions Books Pvt. Ltd.
1711, Centre 1, World Trade Centre,
Cuffe Parade, Mumbai 400 005, India.

Fill in the Mailing List form on our website
and receive, via email, information on
books, authors, events and more.
Visit: www.yogiimpressions.com

Telephone: (022) 61541500, 61541541
E-mail: yogi@yogiimpressions.com

 Join us on Facebook:
www.facebook.com/yogiimpressions

TITLES OF GAUTAM SACHDEVA
PUBLISHED BY YOGI IMPRESSIONS

The End of Separation (2015)

Explosion of Love (2011)

The Buddha's Sword (2009)

Pointers from Ramesh Balsekar (2008)

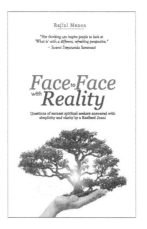

The Sacred India Tarot

Inspired by Indian Mythology and Epics

78 cards + 4 bonus cards + 350 page handbook

The Sacred India Tarot is truly an offering from India to the world. It is the first and only Tarot deck that works solely within the parameters of sacred Indian mythology – almost the world's only living mythology today.

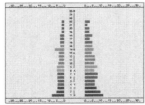
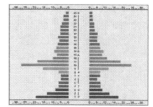

Made in the USA
Lexington, KY
21 March 2018